S0-BOQ-892

ISBN 1 85854 597 8
© Brimax Books Ltd 1997. All rights reserved.
Published by Brimax Books Ltd, Newmarket,
England CB8 7AU 1997.
Printed in France.

I Know my Alphabet

by Gill Davies
Illustrated by Stephanie Longfoot

BRIMAX • NEWMARKET • ENGLAND

The alphabet goes from **a** to **z**.
Letters start every word we use.
This picture is full of things you can find
To match every letter you choose.

Oo Pp Qq Rr Ss Tt Uu Vv Ww Xx Yy Zz

a is for **a**nimals we like to watch,
And **z** is the letter for **z**oo.
How many other words can you find,
With the letters to give you a clue?

Aa Bb

Now I am big I can write my own name
And I know letters like **a** and like **b**.
a is for **a**lphabet shown in the pages
In **b** for the **b**ook on my knee.

Cc

c is for cat asleep on my bed,
Paws neatly tucked under his chest.
With my crayon I draw a big c and a cat.
I like the cat's whiskers the best.

Dd Ee

d is the **d**og who barks on the **d**eck
When we take a trip out on the boat.
e is for **e**ggs the **d**uck guards in her nest
Where the lilies and lily pads float.

Ff

f is for **f**rog and the **f**ish in the lake.
I catch a **f**at **f**ish on my line.
But then put him back, to swim happily off
Where the water is smooth and **f**ine.

Gg Hh

g is for **g**randma we visit one day
When the snow lies thick on the **g**round.
h is for **h**ouse, warm and cosy inside,
While outside the snow whirls around.

Ii Jj

i is the igloo we build from the snow,
Until grandma says, "Come inside, please."
j is the jam she spreads on our bread,
As our toes and our fingers unfreeze.

Kk Ll

k is for kite that we fly in the fields
and l is for lamb that is shy.
Stopping and staring, running to mother,
To peep as the kite rises high.

Mm Nn

m is for **m**an who is driving a tractor.
Chug! Chug! to the field's furthest edge.
n is for **n**est where baby birds cheep.
Their beaks open wide in the hedge.

Oo Pp

o is an ogre in a puppet show play
And p is the prince in the play.
He lives in a palace with q for the queen
Who wears a big crown every day.

r is the **r**ing that is magic, of course,
And so helps the **p**rince become king.
The **p**lay makes us happy; we clap and we cheer,
We shout and we laugh and we sing.

Ss Tt

s is for stores when we're shopping in town.
I like the stores with toys,
Especially trucks and teddy bears
And trains that make a noise.

We buy an **u**mbrella and a **v**ase,
And **v**egetables good to eat.
It is **v**ery hard to carry all these bags
Along this **v**ery crowded **s**treet.

Ww Xx

w is for **w**itch, in a picture at school
Her nose is incredibly long.
And **x** is the letter for **x**ylophone
When we learn about music and song.

Yy Zz

y is for **y**ellow, and **y**ellow's the coat
That I wear on a **w**inter's day.
z is for **z**ipper that **z**ips up my coat
When I go to the playground to play.